This Sermon Journal Belongs To:

_____

Matthew 5:13-16

"You are the salt of the earth, but if the salt has lost its flavor,
with what will it be salted?
It is then good for nothing, but to be cast out and trodden
under the feet of men.
You are the light of the world.
A city located on a hill can't be hidden.
Neither do you light a lamp, and put it under a measuring basket,
but on a stand; and it shines to all who are in the house.

Date

Title/Topic

Speaker

Scripture References

Main Theme

Key Points

Key Words

Notes

_____

Further Study

Date —————————— Speaker ——————————
Title/Topic ——————————————————

Scripture References

Main Theme

Key Points

Key Words

Notes

_____
_____
_____
_____
_____
_____
_____
_____
_____
_____
_____
_____
_____
_____
_____
_____
_____
_____
_____
_____
_____
_____
_____
_____
_____
_____
_____
_____

Further Study

Date ——————————— Speaker ———————————————————

Title/Topic ———————————————————————————————

Scripture References

Main Theme

Key Points

Key Words

Notes

Further Study

Date _____ Speaker _____
Title/Topic _____

Scripture References

Main Theme

Key Points

Key Words

Notes

_____

Further Study

Date ——————————— Speaker ———————————
Title/Topic ————————————————————

Scripture References

Main Theme

Key Points

Key Words

Notes

Further Study

Date —————————— Speaker ——————————————

Title/Topic —————————————————————————

Scripture References

Main Theme

Key Points

Key Words

Notes

_____
_____
_____
_____
_____
_____
_____
_____
_____
_____
_____
_____
_____
_____
_____
_____
_____
_____
_____
_____
_____
_____
_____
_____
_____

Further Study

Date —————————————— Speaker ——————————————————
Title/Topic ——————————————————————————————————

Scripture References ————————————

Main Theme

Key Points

Key Words

Notes

Further Study

Date

Title/Topic

Speaker

Scripture References

Main Theme

Key Points

Key Words

Notes

_____

Further Study

Date —————————— Speaker ——————————————

Title/Topic ——————————————————————————

Scripture References

Main Theme

Key Points

Key Words

Notes

Further Study

Date ——————————— Speaker ———————————

Title/Topic ————————————————————————

Scripture References

Main Theme

Key Points

Key Words

Notes

_____
_____
_____
_____
_____
_____
_____
_____
_____
_____
_____
_____
_____
_____
_____
_____
_____
_____
_____
_____
_____
_____
_____
_____
_____
_____
_____
_____
_____
_____
_____
_____
_____

Further Study

Date ————————— Speaker ———————————————

Title/Topic ——————————————————————————

Scripture References

Main Theme

Key Points

Key Words

Notes

_____
_____
_____
_____
_____
_____
_____
_____
_____
_____
_____
_____
_____
_____
_____
_____
_____
_____
_____
_____
_____
_____
_____
_____
_____
_____

Further Study

Date —————— Speaker ——————————————

Title/Topic ——————————————————

Scripture References

Main Theme

Key Points

Key Words

Notes

Further Study

Date ——————— Speaker ————————————

Title/Topic ———————————————————

Scripture References

Main Theme

Key Points

Key Words

Notes

_____
_____
_____
_____
_____
_____
_____
_____
_____
_____
_____
_____
_____
_____
_____
_____
_____
_____
_____
_____
_____
_____
_____
_____
_____

Further Study

Date ———————————— Speaker ————————————

Title/Topic ————————————

Scripture References

Main Theme

Key Points

Key Words

Notes

_____
_____
_____
_____
_____
_____
_____
_____
_____
_____
_____
_____
_____
_____
_____
_____
_____
_____
_____
_____
_____
_____
_____
_____
_____
_____
_____
_____

Further Study

Date —————— Speaker ——————

Title/Topic ——————

Scripture References

Main Theme

Key Points

Key Words

Notes

_____

_____

_____

_____

_____

_____

_____

_____

_____

_____

_____

_____

_____

_____

_____

_____

_____

_____

_____

_____

_____

_____

_____

_____

_____

_____

_____

_____

_____

Further Study

Date ——————— Speaker ———————————————

Title/Topic ——————————————————————————

Scripture References

Main Theme

Key Points

Key Words

Notes

Further Study

Date ————— Speaker —————
Title/Topic —————

Scripture References

Main Theme

Key Points

Key Words

Notes

_____
_____
_____
_____
_____
_____
_____
_____
_____
_____
_____
_____
_____
_____
_____
_____
_____
_____
_____
_____
_____
_____
_____
_____
_____
_____
_____
_____
_____

Further Study

Date ———————— Speaker ————————————
Title/Topic ———————————————————————

Scripture References

Main Theme

Key Points

Key Words

Notes

_____
_____
_____
_____
_____
_____
_____
_____
_____
_____
_____
_____
_____
_____
_____
_____
_____
_____
_____
_____
_____
_____
_____
_____
_____
_____
_____
_____
_____
_____
_____
_____

Further Study

Date ————————— Speaker ——————————————

Title/Topic ————————————————————————————

Scripture References

Main Theme

Key Points

Key Words

Notes

Further Study

Date ——————— Speaker ———————
Title/Topic ———————

Scripture References

Main Theme

Key Points

Key Words

Notes

Further Study

Date ——————— Speaker ——————————
Title/Topic ———————————————

Scripture References

Main Theme

Key Points

Key Words

Notes

Further Study

Date ——————————— Speaker ———————————

Title/Topic ———————————

Scripture References

Main Theme

Key Points

Key Words

Notes

_____
_____
_____
_____
_____
_____
_____
_____
_____
_____
_____
_____
_____
_____
_____
_____
_____
_____
_____
_____
_____
_____
_____
_____
_____
_____

Further Study

Date —————————— Speaker ————————————

Title/Topic ————————————————————————

Scripture References

Main Theme

Key Points

Key Words

Notes

Further Study

Date _____ Speaker _____

Title/Topic _____

Scripture References

Main Theme

Key Points

Key Words

Notes

Further Study

Date ———————— Speaker —————————

Title/Topic ——————————————————————

Scripture References

Main Theme

Key Points

Key Words

Notes

_____
_____
_____
_____
_____
_____
_____
_____
_____
_____
_____
_____
_____
_____
_____
_____
_____
_____
_____
_____
_____
_____
_____
_____
_____

Further Study

Date————————— Speaker —————————

Title/Topic—————————

Scripture References

Main Theme

Key Points

Key Words

Notes

Further Study

Date ————————— Speaker ————————————————
Title/Topic ——————————————————————————

Scripture References

Main Theme

Key Points

Key Words

Notes

_____

Further Study

Date _____ Speaker _____

Title/Topic _____

Scripture References

Main Theme

Key Points

Key Words

Notes

Further Study

Date —————————— Speaker ——————————
Title/Topic ——————————————————

Scripture References

Main Theme

Key Points

Key Words

Notes

Further Study

Date _____ Speaker _____
Title/Topic _____

Scripture References

Main Theme

Key Points

Key Words

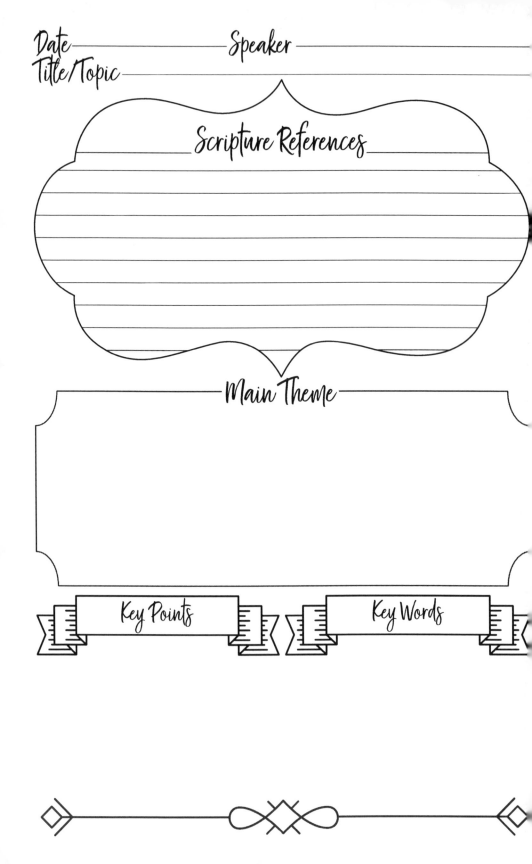

Notes

_____

Further Study

Date ———————— Speaker ————————
Title/Topic ————————

Scripture References

Main Theme

Key Points

Key Words

Notes

_____

Further Study

Date _____ Speaker _____
Title/Topic _____

Scripture References

Main Theme

Key Points

Key Words

Notes

_____

Further Study

Date —————————— Speaker ——————————
Title/Topic ——————————

Scripture References

Main Theme

Key Points

Key Words

Notes

Further Study

Date ——————————————— Speaker ———————————————
Title/Topic ———————————————

Scripture References

Main Theme

Key Points

Key Words

Notes

_____

_____

_____

_____

_____

_____

_____

_____

_____

_____

_____

_____

_____

_____

_____

_____

_____

_____

_____

_____

_____

_____

_____

_____

_____

_____

_____

_____

Further Study

Date ————————————— Speaker ——————————————
Title/Topic ———————————————————————————

Scripture References

Main Theme

Key Points

Key Words

Notes

_____

Further Study

Date —————————— Speaker ————————————

Title/Topic ——————————————————

Scripture References

Main Theme

Key Points

Key Words

Notes

_____
_____
_____
_____
_____
_____
_____
_____
_____
_____
_____
_____
_____
_____
_____
_____
_____
_____
_____
_____
_____
_____
_____
_____
_____
_____
_____

Further Study

Date —————————— Speaker ——————————————

Title/Topic ——————————————————————

Scripture References ————————

Main Theme ————

Key Points

Key Words

Notes

_____
_____
_____
_____
_____
_____
_____
_____
_____
_____
_____
_____
_____
_____
_____
_____
_____
_____
_____
_____
_____
_____
_____
_____
_____
_____
_____
_____

Further Study

Date ———————————— Speaker ————————————

Title/Topic ————————————

Scripture References

Main Theme

Key Points

Key Words

Notes

_____

Further Study

Date
Title/Topic

Speaker

Scripture References

Main Theme

Key Points

Key Words

Notes

Further Study

Date ———————————————— Speaker ————————————————

Title/Topic ————————————————

Scripture References

Main Theme

Key Points

Key Words

Notes

_____
_____
_____
_____
_____
_____
_____
_____
_____
_____
_____
_____
_____
_____
_____
_____
_____
_____
_____
_____
_____
_____
_____
_____
_____
_____
_____

Further Study

Date ———————————— Speaker ————————————
Title/Topic ————————————

Scripture References

Main Theme

Key Points

Key Words

Notes

_____

_____

_____

_____

_____

_____

_____

_____

_____

_____

_____

_____

_____

_____

_____

_____

_____

_____

_____

_____

_____

_____

_____

_____

_____

_____

_____

_____

Further Study

Date —————————— Speaker ——————————
Title/Topic ——————————————————————

Scripture References

Main Theme

Key Points

Key Words

Notes

Further Study

Date ———————————— Speaker ————————————

Title/Topic ————————————

Scripture References

Main Theme

Key Points

Key Words

Notes

_____

_____

_____

_____

_____

_____

_____

_____

_____

_____

_____

_____

_____

_____

_____

_____

_____

_____

_____

_____

_____

_____

_____

_____

_____

_____

_____

_____

Further Study

Date _____ Speaker _____

Title/Topic _____

Scripture References _____

_____
_____
_____
_____
_____
_____
_____
_____
_____

Main Theme

Key Points

Key Words

Notes

_____

Further Study

Date —————————— Speaker ——————————

Title/Topic ——————————

Scripture References

Main Theme

Key Points

Key Words

Notes

Further Study

Date ——————————— Speaker ———————————
Title/Topic ———————————

Scripture References

Main Theme

Key Points

Key Words

Notes

_____
_____
_____
_____
_____
_____
_____
_____
_____
_____
_____
_____
_____
_____
_____
_____
_____
_____
_____
_____
_____
_____
_____
_____
_____
_____
_____
_____
_____
_____

Further Study

Date ——————————— Speaker ———————————

Title/Topic ——————————————————

Scripture References

Main Theme

Key Points

Key Words

Notes

Further Study

Date _____
Title/Topic _____

Speaker _____

Scripture References

Main Theme

Key Points

Key Words

Notes

_____

_____

_____

_____

_____

_____

_____

_____

_____

_____

_____

_____

_____

_____

_____

_____

_____

_____

_____

_____

_____

_____

_____

_____

_____

_____

Further Study

Date _____ Speaker _____
Title/Topic _____

Scripture References

Main Theme

Key Points

Key Words

Notes

Further Study

Matthew 5:13-16

"YOU ARE THE SALT OF THE EARTH, BUT IF THE SALT HAS LOST ITS FLAVOR,
WITH WHAT WILL IT BE SALTED?
IT IS THEN GOOD FOR NOTHING, BUT TO BE CAST OUT AND TRODDEN
UNDER THE FEET OF MEN.
YOU ARE THE LIGHT OF THE WORLD.
A CITY LOCATED ON A HILL CAN'T BE HIDDEN.
NEITHER DO YOU LIGHT A LAMP, AND PUT IT UNDER A MEASURING BASKET,
BUT ON A STAND; AND IT SHINES TO ALL WHO ARE IN THE HOUSE.

Made in the USA
Middletown, DE
21 August 2024

59565021R00057